MOUNTAIN
SAFETY
FOR
KIDS

MOUNTAIN SAFETY FOR KIDS

FIRST EDITION

Copyright © 2018 Rebecca Hinds

Mountain Safety for Kids is written and self-published by the author, Rebecca Hinds.

Edited by Jennifer Sweete with author

Cover Art & Design by Linda McGowan, Copyright © Rebecca Hinds

Illustrated by Linda McGowan, Copyright © Rebecca Hinds

Layout Design by Linda McGowan with author, Copyright © Rebecca Hinds

Paperback
ISBN 13: 978-1717430083
ISBN 10: 1717430082

Dedication page

To my parents who taught me how
to love the mountains

My daughter who shares my love
for the mountains

and

Everyone learning how to
love the mountains

~ Rebecca

For the artists of the world
who love the wild as much as I.

~Linda

MOUNTAIN SAFETY

Stay with your adult in the mountains.
Keep your adult close.

What does your adult look like?
What color shirt is your adult wearing?
What color hair does your adult have? Color your adult.

STAY ON THE TRAIL

Staying on the trail helps keep the mountains beautiful for everyone to enjoy.

Trails are the safest place to hike.
Be sure to stay safe in the mountains!

IF YOU GET LOST

Stay where you are
and wait for someone to find you.

Yell a lot!
Whistle really loud if you can!
Hug a tree and stay in one spot!

CAMPFIRE SAFETY

Make sure to put your campfire out all the way <u>with water</u>
<u>You can!</u> Prevent a forest fire

When you build a fire, use rock rings and fire pits
that are already there.

CAMPFIRE SAFETY

Collect dead wood for campfires.
Trees that are alive
don't make good firewood...

and they make a lot of smoke
when you try to burn them.

CAMPFIRE SAFETY

Be safe and smart around campfires!

Walk slowly around campfires!
Sit and enjoy the fire. Eat s'mores and tell stories.

CAMPFIRE SAFETY

Trash is not okay to burn.
Pack it in, pack it out.

Smoke from burning trash is
not good to breathe.

PACK IT IN, PACK IT OUT

Keep the mountains clean. Pick up your trash.
If you bring it with you, take it home with you.

Circle what does **NOT** belong
in the mountains

BE PREPARED

What are some of the most important things to have with you in the mountains?

Circle what you think is most important
to have in the mountains. Why?

BE PREPARED

The best thing for a kid to have in the mountains is a safety whistle. A safety whistle is NOT a toy!

Safety whistles should only be blown in an emergency! Use it only when you need help or are lost.

BE PREPARED

Good things
for kids to have in the mountains:
1. Whistle
2. Jacket
3. Flashlight
4. Water

The Ten Essentials
for your adult:

1. Water
2. Food
3. First Aid Kit
4. Sunscreen
5. Jacket
6. Multi-tool/knife
7. Flashlight
8. Matches
9. Shelter
10. Compass and Map
    (GPS doesn't work in the mountains)

Does your adult have the 10 essentials?

BE PREPARED

Watch the sky.
The weather can change really quick in the mountains.

Be ready and be prepared.
Do you have your jacket?

BE PREPARED

Can you see in the dark?
Do you have a flashlight?

Have fun with shadow puppets.

BE PREPARED
FOR WILD ANIMALS!

Stay away from wild animals!
Wild animals can be dangerous.

Please DO NOT feed the wild animals.
They are on a special diet.
Feeding wild animals will make them sick.

WILD ANIMALS

Make sure to put your food where
wild animals can't get into it.

Wild animals are out at night and will get into your food
if you leave it out.

WILD ANIMALS
ARE ALL AROUND

These are some of the wild animals
you can see in the mountains.

Circle the wild animals you've seen in the mountains.
Be sure to keep a safe distance from wild animals.

HAVE FUN
IN THE MOUNTAINS

Leave the mountains how you found them
so others can enjoy them too.

Take pictures, not flowers.
The mountains need flower seeds to make more flowers.

WHAT DID YOU LEARN
ABOUT BEING IN THE MOUNTAINS?

MOUNTAIN SAFETY

Should you let your adult wander off without you in the mountains?

☐ yes ☐ no

Is it best to keep your adult close to you in the mountains?

☐ yes ☐ no

STAY ON THE TRAIL

Where is the safest place to hike in the mountains?

☐ on the trail ☐ off the trail

IF YOU GET LOST

What should you do if you get lost?

☐ run in circles ☐ whistle ☐ hide ☐ hug a tree

☐ yell ☐ be quiet ☐ stay in one place

☐ try to find your way home

FIRE SAFETY

What do you need to put a campfire out all the way?

☐ dirt ☐ wood ☐ water ☐ more fire

Where is the best place to build a fire?

☐ anywhere ☐ under a tree ☐ in rock rings and fire pits already there

What kind of firewood should you use for your campfire?

☐ trees that are alive ☐ dead wood

What happens when you burn trees that are alive?

☐ they pop ☐ they smoke a lot

How do you stay safe around a campfire?

☐ sit quietly and tell stories ☐ run around and be crazy

Is it OK to burn trash?

☐ yes ☐ no

Is smoke from burning trash good to breathe?

☐ yes ☐ no

PACK IT IN PACK IT OUT

What should you do with your trash when you're in the mountains?
- ☐ leave it to blow away
- ☐ wait for the animals to pick it up
- ☐ take it home with you

BE PREPARED

Are you prepared to be in the mountains?
- ☐ yes
- ☐ no

What are some important things to have with you in the mountains?
- ☐ gum
- ☐ a puzzle
- ☐ water
- ☐ sleeping bag
- ☐ food
- ☐ crayons
- ☐ shelter

What is the best thing for a kid to have in the mountains?
- ☐ a sandwich
- ☐ a stuffed animal
- ☐ an emergency whistle

Is an emergency whistle a toy?
- ☐ yes
- ☐ no

When should an emergency whistle be used?
- ☐ all the time
- ☐ first thing in the morning
- ☐ only in an emergency

What should a kid have in the mountains?
- ☐ a lego
- ☐ a whistle
- ☐ a jacket
- ☐ a rubber ducky
- ☐ water
- ☐ a flashlight

What should your adult have in the mountains?
- ☐ a cell phone
- ☐ a First Aid kit
- ☐ a small TV
- ☐ twenty bucks
- ☐ sunscreen
- ☐ food and water
- ☐ a multi-tool knife

What do you need when the weather changes in the mountains?
- ☐ a book
- ☐ sunscreen
- ☐ a toy
- ☐ a jacket

Did you make shadow puppets in your tent?
- ☐ yes
- ☐ no

WILD ANIMALS

Are wild animals dangerous?
- ☐ yes
- ☐ no

Is it good to try to pet wild animals?
- ☐ yes
- ☐ no

Are you supposed to feed wild animals?
- ☐ yes
- ☐ no

WILD ANIMALS

Why aren't you supposed to feed wild animals?

☐ they are on a special diet   ☐ it will make them sick

What will wild animals do if you leave your food out when you're camping?

☐ walk on by   ☐ get into it   ☐ call their friends over for a party

☐ eat it   ☐ make a mess

Where is a safe place to put your food so wild animals can't get into it?

☐ in your tent   ☐ in your car   ☐ in a tree

Hint: *It is not safe to keep ANY food in your tent. Wild animals will smell it and try to get into your tent for the food. You do not want to wake up to a bear in your tent!*

Where can you see wild animals?

☐ in the sky   ☐ in trees   ☐ in the creek

☐ in the woods   ☐ on top of a mountain   ☐ all around you

How far are you supposed to stay away from a wild animal?

☐ 1 mile   ☐ 2 miles   ☐ a safe distance

HAVE FUN IN THE MOUNTAINS

What should you do with the beautiful wildflowers in the mountains?

☐ pick them for all your friends   ☐ step on them and squish them

☐ take pictures to share

Why is it important to leave wildflowers where they are?

☐ rocks will get lonely   ☐ bees need them for food

☐ mountains need the seeds to make new flowers

If everyone picked wildflowers, would there be any left?

☐ yes   ☐ no

WHAT WAS THE MOST FUN THING
ABOUT BEING IN THE MOUNTAINS?

Did you have fun in the mountains?

Draw a picture of the most amazing thing you saw in the mountains!

Made in the USA
Columbia, SC
05 June 2018